Love and Roller Coasters:
A Kings Island Memoir

Leigh Harbin

Love and Roller Coasters

DEDICATION

In loving memory of my parents, Bud and Sheila.

Contents

A SOUVENIR PHOTOGRAPH

from

Kings Island

CINCINNATI, OHIO

*Cover and souvenir photo of Leigh and Bud
on the Kings Mills Log Flume c. 1979*

Leigh and Bob, forty years later,
on Race for Your Life Charlie Brown in 2018

EDITOR'S NOTE ON THE PHOTOGRAPHS:
The images from the 1970s are taken from photographs taken by young Leigh. Old Leigh relates, *"I took the pictures of Kings Island included throughout the book sometime between 1974 and 1977 with my own camera, a present from my dad. I wanted to record some of my favorite sights in the park, but I didn't have the patience to take good photos. I did rush when I was taking them because I was too eager to get on the next ride. I do wish I'd gotten somebody to take one of my dad and me together!"*

Entry at the Gate

"Great God! Six bucks," growled my dad. We had finally reached the ticket window.

Bud Harbin, child of the Great Depression, was in a state of outrage.

The afternoon sun was hot. Hours earlier, our long drive from Parkersburg, West Virginia had begun in darkness. We had not stopped for lunch. About an hour ago, I'd caught a glimpse of what appeared to be the top of the Eiffel Tower. I'd been staring at it ever since, as we made our way along unfamiliar roads. What was the Eiffel Tower doing in Southern Ohio? I didn't know, and I really wanted to find out.

It was 1972. Nobody had cell phones. I was ten years old and learning to navigate. I encouraged my dad to

Kings Island Eiffel Tower circa 1974

keep driving toward the tower, hoping we wouldn't get lost. A few days earlier, my dad had announced, "This new park, Kings Island, is supposed to be out of this world! Let's drive over there to Cincinnati and see it."

Neither of us knew our way around the Cincinnati area. Greatly relieved to see signs directing us to Kings Island, we soon found ourselves in an interminable line of cars. Relief turned to impatience. Finally, we entered the biggest parking lot either of us had ever seen. We parked, as directed by the attendant, in a vast section of long rows

named for Scooby Doo. Each row had a number which, in our excitement, we completely ignored. Later on, we would realize the seriousness of that error.

Giddy, we hurried toward a crowd at what looked like a bus stop and waited some more. Eventually a long, open-air conveyance

Kings Island Parking Lot circa 1974

with several cars strung together arrived. We boarded. My excitement grew as we moved slowly toward the distant entry gate. The Eiffel Tower kept getting closer. That shuttle itself was one of the best rides I'd ever been on! We disembarked to enter yet another long line. We waited. Finally, we got to the ticket window, and my dad saw the price: "Great God! Six bucks!"

For an awful moment it seemed certain that we were not going any further because the cost of two tickets, twelve dollars, was so unbelievably high. I froze. I feared my dad would say we had to leave. I waited.

The young woman selling tickets must have been used to this response. Maybe she explained that the price covered all the rides. Maybe my dad wanted to see this place just as badly as I did. Anyway, the miracle happened. Before I had even formulated my protest, let alone begun to make a supporting case, he paid the twelve dollars!

We filed through the gate and took in the unobstructed, highly unlikely view of the Eiffel Tower in Southern Ohio. We stared at shops on International Street

Kings Island International Street and Fountains
about 1974

like those in our imagined versions of France or Spain or Germany and at the enormous fountain spurting towering jets of water. We had no idea what to do first. More miracles: I wasn't talking at all and my dad did not complain about the admission price again, ever.

Gary Wachs, who conceived this place where such miracles occurred daily in 1972, describes the crowds of that opening summer in the documentary film *The Tale of Kings Island*. Wachs remembers: "They paid their money and they walked through there....Their jaws dropped!" Wachs tells the truth.

The park was immaculate, filled with people, sunshine, and color every way you looked. Everything looked beautiful. Some of the rides looked both beautiful and terrifying. Absolutely nothing looked boring.

My dad and I were there when it was brand new, and we were definitely staying.

In 1972, I turned ten on May 20. Kings Island opened its gates to the public on April 29, followed by a Grand Opening on May 27. In 2022, Kings Island turns 50 and I turn 60. This story begins in a time when everybody had about five channels, if they had a TV at all. Nobody had a computer. It ends in a world with a lot more ways to play and to work. Our world sometimes almost seems to be losing track of the fact that play and work are not the same thing. We're trying to find our way out of a long pandemic. We're all really uptight, and with good reason.

But in 1972, just as now, the world was often confusing and scary. It could be hard to distinguish real danger from imagined and hard to know how to stay safe. Then as now, kids and parents, or grown-ups and their spouses, often get their signals crossed. They lose track of how to enjoy just being together. For my dad and me, Kings Island became a magical place to have fun and to face fears.

To this day, walking into Kings Island still has the power to stun me into uncharacteristic silence. My husband Bob experienced this on our first visit to the park together in May of 2018. The park's calming effect on his anxious wife shocked Bob as much as Bud Harbin's opening his wallet had shocked me 46 years earlier.

First Day

That miraculous day, the first of many visits to Kings Island, we had driven all morning and well into the hot afternoon. We listened to country music on the car radio, when we could get a station. Between towns it was mostly just static. My dad's olive green, metallic-sparkle-flecked Gran Torino Sport had no air conditioning. When it got too hot, we rolled down the windows. Then we couldn't hear the radio, even if there was a strong signal. So instead we'd sing. "Raindrops Keep Falling on My Head" was my dad's favorite song. "That 'Raindrops' is beautiful!" he'd say, adding that the song made Burt Bacharach rich and that he wished he had written it himself.

Bud Harbin loved music, playing the mandolin, dancing, talking, and yoga. A World War II veteran who earned a BA in English on the GI bill, he worked as a lab tech, volunteered on a community mental health hotline, enjoyed cooking, and was an amateur hypnotist. He loved using his imagination, and most of all, he loved to write. He wrote poems, short stories, and songs. When I was very young, we made up stories together about a family of beetles who lived in the Pine Needle Forest. He and I were characters in these stories, along with three beetle children named Bonnie, Betsy, and Billy Beetle. In these stories, we took the young Beetles on adventures to visit all our favorite

7

monsters. He never wrote any of these stories down. My dad struggled with his writing, fretting over every word. He was told by some people that he was brilliant and creative, and by others that he was stupid, for most of his life. I believe he had undiagnosed dyslexia and ADHD.

On that first long drive to Kings Island, when we got tired of singing, we talked, very loudly, so as to be heard over the roar from the open windows. We talked about our favorite song lyrics, things we'd read, movies we'd seen, or UFOs and monsters, especially Bigfoot. My mom and dad had divorced three years earlier, when I was seven. Since then, I'd seen my dad mostly on weekends. The best part of the deal was that I got two Christmas trees out of it, one at his apartment and one in the house where I lived with my mom and grandma.

Now Kings Island was about to give Christmas some serious competition for Best Day of the Year. We got a quick bite to eat on International Street and then walked into the "Salt Water Circus" dolphin show, in progress. I had only seen dolphins on TV, but my dad had seen them as they swam alongside the ship he served on in the Navy, in the South Pacific. I wanted to see dolphins in the wild someday. I raised my hand when the trainer asked for a volunteer to come up on stage and be part of the show, but I wasn't picked. Oh well. I watched as the older girl the trainer had chosen came up on stage, and hoped I would be here again and get picked when I was older.

After the dolphin show, we walked under a rainbow arch that said "The Happy Land of Hanna-Barbera," which I mispronounced "Hanna-Barbara." We got in line for a ride called The Enchanted Voyage without having any idea what it was. I later learned that this huge dark ride had been the most expensive ride in the park. We'd had a TV set at home since I was five, but it took me a while to recognize that The Enchanted Voyage was a giant TV. From our place in line, I could see that there were little boats to take us inside this massive ride, and I was a little scared. I thought it might be the kind of ride where things would jump out at me. I spent the time in line examining the boats and trying to figure out how to calculate whether we'd get a red one when our turn came. I don't think we did.

I took this photo while waiting to ride The Enchanted Voyage, no doubt hoping for a red boat.

When we finally floated into the ride, the air conditioning blast felt so good I forgot to be scared. The three-dimensional spectacle of cartoon characters in richly detailed scenes had so much light and activity. I couldn't look closely enough to see everything before something new appeared. The ride featured the Flintstones, Yogi Bear and Boo-Boo, and many other characters. It lasted a long time and had themed sections, including a hillbilly hoe-down, a circus, and a spooky area starring Scooby Doo. This not-too-scary section was my favorite. I never could understand all the words to the ride's theme song, but it wasn't long before I memorized it as best I could. I still remember some of the lyrics, especially the part about how

Bristle Hound always rescued little Lamsey. My dad knew who Fred Flintstone was, but he had never seen most of the others. "Who the hell is Bristle Hound?" "Who is this Scooby Doo?" I thoroughly enjoyed explaining it all to him. He loved The Enchanted Voyage as much as I did. Next, my dad rode the Scooby Doo Coaster,

Kings Island Aerial View
Fred Flintstone circa 1974

having been properly informed about its namesake. I waited for him on a bench. It was supposed to be for kids, but it looked too scary for me.

Moving on to Rivertown, we rode the fantastic Kings Mills Log Flume ride, a totally new experience for us both. Sitting inside a plastic log speeding through a trough high among the trees and ending with a thrilling plunge and a cooling splash felt wonderful. This was my first experience of a roller coaster-style drop, albeit a small one. Refreshed, we moved on.

Surprised to see actors performing a melodrama with a black-hatted villain menacing a girl in a white dress who needed rescuing, just like Snidely Whiplash and Nell

Fenwick, we stopped to watch the show. Then we headed for the KI and Miami Valley Railroad. Four years earlier we'd visited Cedar Point in Northern Ohio. A similar ride there had terrified six-year-old me. I had screamed and tried to hide as cowboys and Indians shot their rifles at each other. This time, however, I was prepared. I knew those guns weren't real. I felt brave and sophisticated.

All my confidence departed, however, when my dad wanted to ride the elevator to the top of the Eiffel Tower. A third the size of the Paris original, the centerpiece of Kings Island provides a stunning view of the park and the surrounding landscape. I loved looking at it from the ground, and I had already begun to try to orient myself in the park by using it as a landmark, but I was terrified to go to the top. We compromised by climbing the stairs to the lower-level observation deck, a challenging task in itself. The view of International Street and the enormous Royal Fountain with its glorious dancing jets of water was well worth it, but I felt nervous even at that height. We walked slowly back down. Then I waited while my dad rode the elevator to the top. He returned, assuring me that the elevator was less scary than the stairs we had just climbed. There were bars taller than he was at the top to keep you from falling, he declared, insisting that I should go up with him. "You've got to try it. There are kids littler than you up there and having a ball! I know you'll love it! You can't fall!" I was not so sure. Nope. Not happening.

We rode more familiar rides like the Scrambler. I adored the speed. I drove the little cars—both the modern sports cars on the Marathon Turnpike and the elegant antique cars. I always hoped for a red one, but no matter what color we got, I still enjoyed the experience. These little cars were harder to drive than our own, real cars: the blue Studebaker Lark, then a big aqua Ford, and now the olive green Gran Torino Sport. I knew because my dad had been letting me drive ever since I was big enough to reach the wheel sitting on his lap. I did not drive as a child on the public streets of Parkersburg; just occasionally on the interstate highway, when I would hold the wheel and steer briefly for my dad if he decided to take off his shirt because it was getting too hot in the car.

I always drove when we visited the flood wall in Parkersburg, a long grassy hill with a flat top. Most people parked on one side of the flood wall, then either climbed over on foot or walked to its gate, and proceeded to the river bank to enjoy a swim in the Ohio River. In my family, though, part of the fun included a drive up the side. It was like a roller coaster, my dad explained. My aunt Jo, my cousins, and my best friend Polly, who lived down the street at her grandmother's house, would usually come along. We all laughed and screamed as I drove the car up the steep slope. We never drove all the way over the top, although I think that may have been my dad's initial goal. The thrill ride became a scientific experiment, trying to determine how far I could steer the car up the side before it began to feel unstable and he would tell me to swerve and drive back down.

On that summer day at Kings Island, not surprisingly, my dad wanted to ride The Racer. However, he didn't get to ride it because it was temporarily closed. Earlier I had heard a couple of older girls shriek "David Cassidy!" as they raced off somewhere. I told my dad the Partridge Family must be in the park. "Who the hell is the Partridge Family?" he demanded. I explained the characters in the TV show and who played each one. He recognized the name of the actress Shirley Jones, and told me which movies he'd seen her in.

Apparently, The Racer was closed for the Partridge Family cast members to ride it. Later, we noticed a huge crowd assembled around a stage near the Royal Fountain to see the Partridge Family perform. I figured famous people probably visited Kings Island often, maybe every day. Later that year when the episode of *The Partridge Family* called "I Left My Heart in Cincinnati" aired, I was thrilled. I never spotted myself nor my dad in the footage, but we were there. I watched them ride The Racer on television long before I got up the nerve to ride it myself.

The Racer is a beautiful double-track coaster. In the book *Kings Island: A Ride Through Time*, Evan Ponstingle tells the terrific story of how Gary Wachs persuaded John Allen, retired president of the Philadelphia Toboggan Company, to come out of retirement to design this ride for Kings Island. The Racer would prove so popular that it inspired a new wave of classic wooden coasters. Neither my dad nor I knew any of this when he rode it for the first time. I don't recall for certain whether he rode it that day, or on another visit, but I do know the line was very long. I settled on a bench and watched this gorgeous ride intensely, trying to pick him out as each train ascended and descended. The cars were too far away and there was no way I could see him.

A few years before, we'd gone to Camden Park in Huntington, West Virginia. I wouldn't ride the Big Dipper coaster there, and The Racer was a whole lot bigger. A pristine white serpent, The Racer wound along the Coney Mall, rising up behind the games and other rides like the pictures of the Loch Ness Monster I'd seen in my dad's *Fate* magazines. I walked along the mall trying to see as much of it as I could, always careful to return to my designated waiting spot. After what seemed like hours, I saw my dad coming out of the exit line, and felt relieved. He was grinning ear to ear. "It's smooth! Not jerky or rough. You've got to try it. There are kids littler than you riding it and having a ball! I know you'll love it! You can't fall!" But he could not convince me to ride The Racer that day.

On our first day at Kings Island, we stayed until after dark and watched the biggest fireworks display we'd ever seen. It was after eleven o'clock when we headed back to the crowded parking lot. That was when we realized that we should have written down the number of the row in which we had parked.

After what seemed like hours of searching, we finally found the Gran Torino, then joined the longest line yet: the one to leave the parking lot. I noticed the adjacent Kings Island Inn, looking as pretty as the buildings on International Street. It might as well have been the Ritz Carlton as far as my dad was concerned. "Let's just go in to look at it," I suggested. Inside the clean, well-lit lobby we saw that the line to check in, while long, was short compared to the wait for the rides or the wait to leave the parking lot. There were several uniformed people helping guests, so it went fast. "How much is a room?" I asked. "Twenty-six dollars a night," replied a pretty, efficient young woman behind the counter. We left. There was not to be another miracle that day.

Back in the car, we began our search for a place to sleep. We were looking for a motel, not a hotel. Hotels were too expensive. My dad thought we'd find better rates farther away from the park. He picked a road and drove. I looked for one with a vacancy, reading the names aloud from the neon signs. Most of the places said "NO VACANCY." After about an hour of this, my dad saw a man walking on the sidewalk and asked me "that guy there, he's white, isn't he?" This bothered me. I watched *Kid Power* on Saturday mornings and I learned from that cartoon that kids of all colors played together, had adventures, solved problems, and got along, and that kids should try to make sure adults did the same. I wanted to ask him what difference it made what color the man I saw on the street was, but I didn't ask him then. I felt very tired and I instinctively avoided questions that might make him defensive.

Eventually we found a motel with a vacancy, where a thin, elderly white man wearing an old white T-shirt sat alone inside a dirty little office smoking a cigarette. The price was right. Our room was dingy but I hadn't stayed in many hotels or motels before, so I wasn't picky. I always loved the little tiny soaps and the machines on the beds called "Magic Fingers." This motel had a Magic Fingers, but oddly, it was on the chair, not the bed. I put in a quarter anyway, and the chair lurched and whirred. One last fun ride to end the day! We got to sleep, probably around three o'clock in the morning.

Kings Island Sky Ride
about 1974

Bumpy Start

Paul aka Bud Harbin
Professional Photo from Olan Mills studio

My dad, Paul James Jackson Harbin, was born in 1925 in Steubenville, Ohio. He was the first child of

Denver Earle and Mabel Louisa. Everybody called him Bud. He had curly reddish-brown hair, sparkling blueish-green eyes, and a great smile.

I liked visiting my grandparents because my Grandma Harbin and I would sit at her kitchen table, eat peanut butter and jelly on saltine crackers, and talk. My Grandpa Harbin was a grouch and a racist. I asked my mom about the N word after hearing him use it while he watched TV. She told me never to say that word because it was a bad word and very hurtful. Grandpa Harbin never seemed happy and I never heard anyone say they liked him. He and my grandmother were married for over 50 years and had five children. My three aunts, Jeannie, Monie, and Joannie, or Jo as we called her, were vivacious women who filled every room they entered with talk and laughter. My Aunt Jo worked as a commercial artist and provided my first role model of a successful career woman who genuinely enjoyed her work. My Uncle Darrell, called Junie, a gifted musician, played guitar, sang, and performed around town.

My Aunt Jo and my mom were good friends in high school. Aunt Jo introduced my parents, stood up at their wedding, and stayed close with both of them after they divorced. She had a gift for diplomacy, if not for matchmaking. My mom and dad were married for ten years before having me. Their divorce made me sad, but it seemed reasonable, as they clearly did not enjoy each other's company. They had frequent loud, heated arguments. My mom cried often. I don't remember my parents ever showing affection for each other or having fun together.

My mom, Sheila, was born in 1933, the only child of Ray and Leone. Her parents divorced when she was young, and her father passed away soon after I was born. Leone was also an only child, making me a third generation only daughter. My mom, a smart, witty, sarcastic, articulate, caring, anxious woman, loved reading, theater, movies, and art. I adored and admired her. She had dark hair, green eyes, and beautiful hands with elegant nails that usually sported a perfect manicure. She took pride in her appearance and her brains, valued friendship and learning very highly, and taught these values to me.

I felt close to my Grandma Leone, but I incorrectly blamed her for my own parents' divorce. She had moved in with us shortly before my dad moved out. She owned a house that had been divided into three apartments, living in one. Moving in with us allowed her to rent all three. Not only did she supplement my mom's income, she was there when I came home from school, and she did a lot of the housework.

In the summer of 1969, when I was seven, my mom announced that she had to tell me something important. We went to her friend Libby's apartment, which had an air conditioner, so we could enjoy the cool air. I guess she thought it would make it easier to talk to me if we were comfortable. She said, "I'm suing your father for divorce." She explained that I should not think the divorce was my fault and that I would still get to spend time with my dad. I was upset, and asked a lot of questions for a long time after that. Our conversation was not like those I saw on the *ABC After School Special* or the *Hallmark Hall of Fame*.

This used to trouble me, but now I think real kids might ask tougher questions than the kids on TV. I asked whether I could choose who I lived with. She said "No." I asked about how much time I would spend with my dad, and where he would live. I learned the name of her lawyer and of my dad's and asked about every step of the process. My mom handled this difficult situation with honesty.

In the end, my mom was awarded a divorce, with no alimony and a weekly child support payment of $27.50. Although this sum bought more groceries in 1969 than it would today, it was by no means generous. She had full custody of me, but she had to allow my dad to see me at "reasonable and seasonable times," such as holidays. My Grandma Leone later told me, no doubt in response to more questions, that she and my mother had made a deal with my dad: they would get the house and me, but he would get the car. My biggest concerns were that I could see my dad whenever I wanted and that our cat, Tabby, would be living with me. Fortunately, both things turned out to be true.

Soon after, my dad took my best friend Polly and me swimming in the Ohio river. It was Labor Day weekend, the last day of summer. Polly and I were wading into the river, barely above our knees, but far from the bank, when suddenly we were both sinking. That river bed had holes, and we had fallen into one. We gasped and bobbed and I started grabbing at Polly, pushing her under. I looked at the river bank, which seemed very far off. My dad was standing on that bank, looking at us, and grinning ear to ear.

In years since, as adults, Polly and I have discussed this event, and she remembers it as I do. I've read that when a person is drowning, it's not all that easy for an observer to tell what's going on, and often they don't react in time. A group of teenage kids were also at the river that day and they were the ones who noticed our struggling. They formed a line, like a bucket brigade, then grabbed us and passed us back to the riverbank. I think my dad began to understand then that we'd been in serious trouble. He thanked the older kids and looked embarrassed. On the way home, he told me not to tell my mom what had happened, because if I did, I wouldn't get to see him again.

He dropped me off at home, the house he had recently moved out of. I went inside and immediately told my mom exactly what had happened. She sat me on her lap, gave me a big hug, and told me that she didn't want to stop me from going places with my dad, so, from now on, I was going to have to be extra careful and look out for my own safety when I was with him. So that was what I did.

Polly and I started second grade the next day, at the same school, but in different classes. I adored my new teacher. I decided my dad should marry her, so I took him to her house, where she lived with her sister. I introduced them and they invited us in for a short visit. Sadly, it was not love at first sight and nothing more came of it.

That year, my dad and I settled into a routine. He would pick me up on Friday nights and take me to dinner at Shoney's or the Wilmar Cafeteria. I looked forward to these dinners and always dressed up. On the weekends my dad would often take Polly and me to the DuPont Employees Recreation Park, which had a wonderful pool. He worked at the DuPont Washington Works plant, the focus of the movie *Dark Waters* and the documentary *The Devil You Know,* about the pollution and disease caused by the carcinogenic chemical C8. In those days, though, a visit to the DuPont Park and its pool was a fabulous treat for us.

After the river incident, my mom insisted I take swimming lessons at the local City Park Pool. I hated those lessons. I didn't understand what the teacher meant when she used certain terms, like when she asked everyone if we could do a "crawl" without explaining that this was the name of a swimming stroke. I also had a lot of trouble learning to breathe the way she instructed us, rotating my head and taking a breath on each side. In the end, I dropped out of the lessons, but my mom would only let me quit if I promised to learn to swim the length of the pool. My dad and I made sure I did. By the end of the summer, I could swim the length of the DuPont pool several times over, and Polly and I were diving down into the deep end to retrieve pennies thrown in by my dad.

Once Polly and I took over my dad's kitchen to cook dinner. It took a long time. We dirtied every dish in his cupboards. My dad didn't eat meat, so we made macaroni and cheese and lots of vegetables. He did not seem to mind the mess at all. He was so impressed that he wrote a poem about the dinner we had cooked, in which he described looking under the table to see if we'd hidden a chef under there.

His dietary choice arose from his interest in eastern religions. My dad's fascination with Buddhism and Hinduism made him stand out at work. The guys he worked with took to calling him "Buddha," shortening it to "Bood," as distinct from Bud. If we ran into them downtown or at the mall, they'd call out, "Hey, Bood" by way of a greeting. While his ideas amused his friends, they hadn't endeared him to my mom. She complained about his righteous refusal to kill insects, even when the house was infested with termites. She was puzzled by his yoga. Once she walked into a dark interior room of the house to tell him something very important, only to realize that she was speaking urgently to his feet because he was standing on his head.

A year or two after the divorce, he decided he wanted to move out of his apartment, and he bought a trailer. He asked me what color he should paint it. I suggested light purple on the top half and dark purple on the bottom. He went along with the idea, so his trailer really stood out. One of the first things my dad did in his new home was buy some silver reflecting tape with adhesive on the back, the kind that bicyclists put on their bikes for nighttime safety. He cut out several odd, shiny shapes, each about as big as a quarter. He placed one above the window in the living room at the front of the trailer, adding more at intervals every few feet, with the last one over his bed at the very back of the trailer. When Polly and I asked him about these homemade decals, he explained that they were letters in the Sanskrit alphabet. He had placed them as a trail to guide his astral body, so that when it left him at night during his astral projection sessions, it would be able to find its way home.

Polly lived with her grandmother, who, luckily for me, had moved to the same trailer park as my dad, so I could walk over to their trailer to visit. There were a lot of stray cats around, and we wanted to make friends with all of them. Polly and I coaxed them with food and brought them into the trailer, then went out looking for more. We wanted to see how many cats we could collect. Sometimes we had twelve or fourteen cats inside the trailer at once. We named them all: Edgar, Goldie, Rasputin and Puff were among our favorites. We loved them all, but fluffy, sweet-natured little Puff, with her big eyes and her coat colored in more shades of gray than seemed possible, became part of the family. My dad often said "That cat is the only one who can live with me." And so she did, for many years, until he took her on a trip with him and lost her at a highway rest stop. I was an adult by then, and furious with him for carelessly thinking he could let a cat out of his sight in a strange place. He never really got over the loss of poor Puff. He wrote a poem about it:

Puff

When my stone-deaf old gray cat got lost
In the savage mountains of Hawk's Nest
My anxious body turned all night and tossed
From feline sadness clawing at my chest.
She was so senile she befriended birds.
She was so human she became a coward.

She was so catless she respected words
More than the perfume that a tomcat showered.
9-Lives and prednisone became her meal.
Hairballs roamed the house like tumbleweed.
Her independence starved into an eel
That wrapped my legs in syncopated greed.
When all the years can so destroy a cat
Where will tomorrow peg to hang my hat?

Up the Lift Hill

My dad and I went back to Kings Island in 1973, 1974, and 1975. Sometimes we brought cousins and aunts. I liked all of them, but their presence meant I had to share my dad's attention with another adult. I liked it best when Polly came with us. She made everything more fun. I continued to avoid the roller coasters and the top of the Eiffel Tower for a very long time. Yet although these attractions scared me, I felt safer at Kings Island than I did most other places.

We managed to get lost on almost every one of these long drives. Once we took a wrong turn and went for miles north and east before we figured out we were lost. I finally noticed that we were mistakenly headed for Youngstown. "No damned signs," my dad growled. We'd get tired and frustrated. I read maps and watched for road signs, but my navigational skills were still only marginally better than my dad's. Often the car broke down and we'd have to get it fixed, losing hours. I was a teenager before I realized that everyone did not typically break down or get lost when they went on road trips.

One summer, instead of heading to Ohio to visit Kings Island, we went instead to Virginia to visit its new sister park, Kings Dominion. Polly came with us. Arriving in Richmond, we drove around for a long time lost downtown and finally found the Edgar Allan Poe house and museum. I was obsessed with Poe, reading his stories, memorizing his poems, and watching all the Vincent Price movies that shared the titles of his works but told completely different stories. I had a powerful crush on Vincent Price from the time I was about six years old. (My dad often took me to see his movies at the drive-in, but he preferred the "true" accounts of ghosts, UFOs, and sightings of Bigfoot or Nessie or Yeti we read in his *Fate* magazines.) We toured the Poe house and marveled at a huge stuffed raven on a perch. After checking out all the books and pictures in the gift shop, we got on the road again, heading for Virginia Beach.

There, I saw the ocean for the first time. The sand felt burning hot on my bare feet and had so many cigarette butts in it, I felt like I was running through a giant ashtray, but I forgot all about the litter once we were in the ocean. My dad taught Polly and me how to dive into the breakers and ride the rolling waves. He stuck pretty close to us that day. The ocean felt like a pool and a roller coaster combined. We ate lunch at a big outdoor restaurant on the beach. My dad and I ate crab legs, which looked like huge bug legs but tasted delicious dipped in melted butter. Polly opted for a hot dog.

Back on the road, a big rainstorm came up suddenly and my dad lost control of the car. Polly and I sat terrified as we slid between the lanes of the interstate. Luckily, we did not collide with any other cars. After a few seconds my dad regained control. He explained to us that we had just "hydroplaned." Always good to learn a new word. I never forgot that one.

We got to Williamsburg in one piece, but couldn't find a restaurant or a hotel that my dad approved. Too expensive. We were all getting pretty hungry, so he finally stopped at a restaurant with the words "dining" and "cocktails" on its sign. Inside, we faced white table cloths and waiters. We were accustomed to plastic booths, Formica tables, and waitresses. We all ordered spaghetti, the cheapest item on the menu, ate it, and left as fast as we could. It tasted good and we were no longer hungry, but this was not a relaxed meal. "No more of these cocktail houses," my dad declared as soon as we returned to the car.

My dad hadn't booked a hotel ahead, thinking we would just find a Days Inn, the only hotel chain with rates he approved. We searched for some time. He finally asked a man at a gas station, who didn't know of any Days Inns in the area, but told him that a local college rented out rooms in their residence halls to travelers. It took a long time to find these dorms. When we finally got there, we were told that Polly and I would have to stay in one building, and my dad would have to stay in another. But it was getting late and the price was right.

My dad was allowed to take us to our room, but then he had to leave. Furthermore, the bathrooms were down the hall! Polly and I were apprehensive and giggly. Suddenly, he told us loudly "Stop that!" "Stop what?" we asked, confused. He growled, "Making fun of me." We protested that we were not making fun of him, which was true.

We were making fun of the odd room with no phone or TV. He left, still huffy. Feeling guilty and muddled, Polly and I took turns going to the bathroom, then we went to bed.

The next morning all this was forgotten as we entered Kings Dominion, which had an Eiffel Tower just like Kings Island. Kings Dominion went deeper into the European theme. A theater that resembled Shakespeare's Globe was my favorite attraction. What we saw there wasn't a real Shakespeare play, but the skits had some Shakespearean references. We took a boat ride down a river pretending to be the Rhine, but nothing happened during it. My dad rode a big roller coaster that neither Polly nor I would ride, and we ate in a German-themed restaurant that featured a very tall layered cake. I wouldn't go to the top of this Eiffel Tower, either. We were glad to have visited Kings Dominion. The next day, we visited Colonial Williamsburg before heading home, without any more hydroplaning.

We returned to Kings Island later that summer and for the next few years. On one of these trips, I finally rode The Racer. I may have been humiliated into taking that first ride by my dad's continual reminders that smaller kids were riding it and having a ball, but I truly did want to ride that terrible, gorgeous white serpent. As we sped down the first drop, I tightened my grip on my dad's arm until I nearly broke it. Then I realized he was right. I loved the speed. I had ridden my first real coaster, and I had to ride it again. And again. It was then, and still is today after renovation in 2020-2021, exactly as my dad described it: just like a flying carpet.

My Aunt Jo joined us on one visit. She was impressed by Kings Island, commenting on how clean it was. In those days, there were fewer safety restrictions, and when we rode the Racer, she and I took our purses, tucking them into the front of the car, down by our feet. Aunt Jo was a very petite lady, and as the ride hurled us forward, she seemed to be trying to push herself down into the nose of the car near our purses. What could she want from her purse so badly in the middle of the ride? She told me later that, in spite of the lap bar, she had been convinced she was going to fly right out of the car. I found it incredible to think that she had been scared. Had I really felt less afraid than my grown-up aunt?

It's the Climb

Polly and I went to different junior high schools, and I didn't make new friends at first. I was a geeky kid with thick glasses and a loud nervous laugh. One day in September, after I had finished eating my lunch alone, a girl I knew from my elementary school came over to me and told me to go with her to the girls' locker room. She wouldn't tell me why. Curious, I followed her downstairs, where a group of girls I didn't know at all surrounded me, making fists and calling me names. I ran right between two of them, back up the stairs and to the main office. The Vice Principal sent me back to class. I finished the school day, then went home and informed my mom I would not go back to school. I tried to talk her into letting me switch to the private Catholic School. She said that I wouldn't learn to deal with the real world in a private school, and that I had to return to school the next day, pretend not to be scared, and tough it out.

So, I did just that, feeling petrified every day for a week. She was right. Nothing else happened.

That Friday, my dad called to cancel our usual Friday night dinner. Disappointed, I told him about my week. He encouraged me. I just needed to get along with the girls I was still afraid of, he said, advising me to "play their ball or whatever." This felt to me like he just didn't get it. They hadn't asked me to play ball, they had threatened to punch me. Nonetheless, he wouldn't change his plans. He needed to get out more and go dancing. I was disappointed and jealous because as far as I was concerned, his weekends were mine. That evening, my mom encouraged me to call some girls and invite them to go roller skating. To my surprise, that also worked. She picked up about five girls and took us to the skating rink for a couple of hours, then took everyone home. Slowly, I made some new friends.

After that, the regular Friday dinners and the weekend overnights with my dad became less frequent. My dad never remarried, but he did plenty of dancing. My mom dated several boring men, then she got serious about Allen Ross, a recently divorced Jewish man originally from the Bronx. Al seemed very capable and sophisticated to me. He was an only child, like my mom and me. A veteran of the Army Corps of Engineers serving in the Korean War, he had been a chemical engineer, but decided he'd prefer to become a salesman because he loved to travel. He drove to regular customers in several states selling hot stamping foil, a product used on labels, book covers, and greeting cards. It looked like gold leaf, but came in every color of the rainbow.

I spent more weekends with my mom and her new boyfriend. Al loved to cook out, marinating and grilling meats. He made tempura, Japanese fried vegetables which I had never heard of, but enjoyed. He also loved restaurants.

In the late 1970s, Parkersburg had an Italian restaurant, a Greek restaurant, a Crêperie, a Chinese restaurant, a Mexican restaurant, and a handful of more formal dining establishments with white table cloths. I was thrilled to enjoy them all with Mom and Al on weekends. His daughter, Elizabeth, lived with her mom. She was three years younger than I and often spent weekends with us. I remember the four of us enjoying the atmospheres and flavors of all these restaurants to this day. I suggested to my dad we try some of them. We did, but he didn't like them. He enjoyed homestyle American food or, once in a while, pizza.

My dad and I still took our summer trips to Kings Island, watching it change. Lion Country Safari became a new favorite. We'd always head there first to get in line for the futuristic monorail ride where we could see giraffes, lions, and tigers. Other new rides came, and the shows changed, but our favorite rides didn't. Every time we drove out of the park at the end of the day, I would look out the back window to see the top of the Eiffel Tower for as long as I could, feeling sad when I couldn't see it anymore.

In 1976, our country celebrated its Bicentennial. That summer, my dad and I hit the road to Disney World in Orlando, Florida, the longest trip we ever made together. I was 14 and he was 50. We left very early and drove from Parkersburg all the way to Atlanta on the first day. We ate pecan pie at Stuckey's. I drank my first coffee and enjoyed my first caffeine buzz, to my dad's delight. Drinking coffee conferred a sort of honorary adult status.

We drove all day, arriving in the early evening at a Days Inn in Georgia. My dad had booked ahead! In the big outdoor pool packed full of kids, I met a girl named Emily from Massachusetts and we were great friends for about half an hour. Having dinner in the Tasty World restaurant, he and I argued about how to spend the rest of our evening. I wanted us to talk. He didn't have a TV in his trailer, so he wanted to watch the one in the room. What I really wanted was for him to make up stories for me, as he had when I was younger. I knew I was too old for that, so I didn't tell him the truth. Instead, I just kept arguing. "What the hell's wrong with wanting to watch a little TV once in a while?" he demanded.

On that epic journey we went on to argue about where to eat, what hotels to stay in, where to get ice cream, and what shows to see in the Magic Kingdom. He wanted to see the dancing saloon girls and I wanted to see the singing Hillbilly Bears. We spent four days at Disney World so we had plenty of time to do both, but we argued anyway. By the end of our stay, I had a sore throat. We blamed it on an allergy to orange blossoms, but it was probably from too much arguing.

I rode It's a Small World alone, because my dad said he had no interest, despite its promise of air conditioning. I boarded the little boat, and about five minutes into the ride, it stopped. After about 25 minutes trapped listening to the song repeat, I realized I needed to pee. Finally, my boat began to move. I liked the idea of this ride: that we all needed to learn to get along. While I understood world unity to be a more noble theme than the adventures of my favorite cartoon characters, I just didn't feel the same love for It's a Small World that I felt for Kings Island's The Enchanted Voyage. I teared up listening to that ride's song about the friends who live in my TV. If I'd been stuck on The Enchanted Voyage, I would have been grateful, because it was always over too soon.

Now a veteran of The Racer, I rode Space Mountain, even though I was scared. The lights and speed of my first metal coaster, and my first indoor one as well, thrilled me. After riding it, I felt ready for anything. The Haunted Mansion, though, with its spooky comic theatrics, was my favorite attraction. We both liked the 20,000 Leagues Under the Sea submarine ride, Pirates of the Caribbean, and the climb into the Swiss Family Robinson's Treehouse, despite the long lines and sweltering heat. Disney World's Bicentennial fireworks, we agreed, made the most incredible display we had ever seen. We got lost in the Magic Kingdom a lot, getting our bearings about the time we were ready to leave.

We left Orlando to explore the state further and ended up yelling at each other in our hotel room at Daytona Beach. I thought the hotel he'd chosen was dumpy, and said so. He asked how I had gotten such fancy tastes. He stormed out of the room and didn't come back for a long time. I waited, beginning to wonder whether he would come back at all. Should I go to the front office and ask if I could make a long-distance call to my mom? I was about to do so, when he returned, much calmer. We went to Red Lobster that night, a surprising choice for him. I tried lobster for the first time. We had a very nice dinner, and there were no more arguments on the way home.

We made a second trip that summer, back to Kings Island, because we both missed it. I gleefully rode The Racer, but I still wouldn't go to the top of the Eiffel Tower. I sat on a bench at its base eating an enormous red, white, and blue Bicentennial popsicle. It didn't taste as good as it looked. By the time my dad came back the popsicle had become a drippy mess. I thought he had stayed away too long. He thought I should have gone with him. After all, there were little tiny kids at the top! How could I still be afraid? "I know you'll love it," he insisted. "You can't fall!" But I wasn't going up there. My Dad and I didn't take a summer trip in 1977 or in 1978. We didn't see each other much at all.

Lost and Found

Al Ross became my stepfather in January 1978. After he and my mom got married, we moved to a nicer house, where I had a prettier bedroom. Polly, whose grandmother had died, lived with us for a year, much to my delight. It felt like I had a sister in the house, which was especially nice because once Mom and Al got settled in, they started arguing as often and as loudly as my mom and dad had.

Al scheduled me for driving lessons with a professional teacher, a seasoned instructor who had already taught his two older sons. After giving me one lesson, the teacher retired. I suspect

Sheila and Allen Ross
Wedding picture 1978

that everything I'd learned from my Dad while driving up and down the side of the flood wall had something to do with his decision. Unphased, Al just hired another teacher. I soon had my license and got to drive Al's old Volvo, a marvelously safe car that felt like a little tank.

In the summer of 1979, between my junior and senior years of high school, Mom and Al announced to Polly, Elizabeth, and me, that they wanted to take a family vacation. They asked where we wanted to go. I suggested New York City. I wanted to go back after having been there on a school trip. Elizabeth wanted to see the hit musical *Annie*. A petite redheaded kid with a belting voice, it was her dream role. Al wasn't enthusiastic, because he thought NYC was dangerous, but he agreed. Mom, Al, Elizabeth, Polly, and I, along with all our luggage, crammed into Al's big sedan. The car made the entire trip without a single breakdown.

At one point, Al wasn't sure where the on ramp to the interstate was, and he began singing, "Where the hell's the highway," to the tune of "She'll Be Coming Round the Mountain." Before he was through making up his song, he'd found the interstate and we were on our way. I had thought it would be hours. Furthermore, Al never asked me to read the map!

Our first stop on this trip was Hershey Park. Our day there turned out to be a wet one. Our group immediately split up. While everyone else hid out from the rain in shops and shows and ate as much chocolate as possible, I systematically rode everything in sight. The rain kept the lines short, but I was the only one who cared. After having ridden The Racer and Space Mountain, I tried all the wooden and steel coasters at this new, chocolaty park. I even rode a coaster that sped through a flaming loop! Oddly, I felt less scared riding alone, but I missed discussing the rides with my dad.

Next, we headed on to New York City. Al booked all the hotels ahead, and if they didn't meet his expectations, he simply insisted on different accommodations. I learned this when we arrived in a hotel just outside the city to discover several ladies wearing a lot of make-up and very high heels standing outside. Al angrily told us all to stay in the car. He came back out quickly and told us he'd demanded that the desk change our reservation to another hotel. I had no idea it was that simple! We just drove for another hour to a different hotel. For years he talked about his dismay at arriving at that hotel with his wife and three teenage girls in the car and we all roared with laughter.

Over a three-day stay in New York, we visited many neighborhoods and saw two Broadway musicals. Al clearly felt nervous taking his new wife and three teenage girls to the city, yet the car had not broken down once and he had only been lost for about ten minutes. He puzzled and impressed me. After that trip, I listened and learned from everything he did.

For example, the first time I flew, I traveled alone to visit a prospective college campus. Al drove me to the airport, reassured me, and gave me great advice. I never flew with my dad, but when I told him I was going to fly, he said, "I hope to God the plane doesn't crash." As an adult, I have traveled on my own in the United States and abroad, despite my anxiety, thanks to Al. I will always be grateful for what he taught me.

It's taken me a while to realize that getting lost with my dad taught me that I could passably read a map, and if we messed up the first time, we could figure it out on the second or third try. We'd have fun on the way, and eventually we always got somewhere.

Later that same summer, my dad once again heard about something new in Cincinnati that was "out of this world." He said we had better drive over to Kings Island to try out this mysterious new ride and I agreed. It had been a couple of years since we'd made a trip together. The TV advertisements set out to make The Beast sound utterly terrifying: a spooky cartoon showed cars on a track propelled by a roaring speed demon phantom, while a horror movie-style voice-over promised that you would scream in terror on this highest, fastest, biggest roller coaster ever. No pictures of the actual ride were shown.

My dad now had a cherry red Camaro. He invited me to take the wheel and provided coaching. "Your driving is fine. I don't see anything wrong with it. Just don't look at the road too much, because it might hypnotize you. If you fall into a trance, you will run us off the road for sure. Better to look around and enjoy conversation or the scenery. And don't be like these women drivers who insist on keeping both hands on the wheel all the time. Relax. Use one hand. Driving should be a pleasure." Somehow, we made it.

This time, I drove into the Kings Island parking lot and noted the number and row of our parking spot. We went to the Dolphin Show, and I hoped I might get chosen when the trainer asked for a volunteer, because I was older, but I didn't. I still adored The Enchanted Voyage, the Kings Mills Log Flume, and The Racer. On this trip, I finally joined my dad at the top of the Eiffel Tower. I thought I was ready for anything.

The line for The Beast was three hours long. The Beast, built into the contours of a tree-lined ravine, was then and remains today the longest wooden roller coaster in the world, at 7,359 feet. I couldn't see any of the ride. We chatted, ran out of things to say, and waited. We watched other people in line, the trees, and the seemingly endless turns and reversals in the neatly cordoned off line.

By the time we got to the boarding area, I was ready to flee. But I heard my dad's words from years before in my mind: "Leigh, you've got to try it. There are littler kids than you riding it and having a ball! It's out of this world." So, I forced myself into the car and pushed the lap bar as tight as it would go. Going up the eternal incline, my dad admired the view. I couldn't believe how high we were. I thought about how new the ride was. Sometimes rides broke and people died. Oh, this had been a mistake. As we reached the summit, I knew this was NOT like The Racer or anything else I'd ever ridden.

As we crested the hill, I felt sure I was flying out of the seat. I grabbed my dad's arm with one hand and the lap bar with the other. I was certainly going to fall. If I didn't fly out of the ride, then we would soon collide with the tiny opening of the dark tunnel we were hurtling toward. I closed my eyes. I opened them somewhere in the dark tunnel, realizing we were alive and still moving very fast. Then there was light, and green, and, sure enough, the feeling of flying through the tree tops on a magic carpet. It went on and on and on through the woods, and it was over too soon.

So, we got in line again. After waiting a few more hours for our second ride on The Beast, I didn't close my eyes. I watched as we flew into the tiny tunnel. Instead of gripping for dear life and holding myself rigid, I relaxed into the experience, felt the weightlessness, and, as my dad would put it, discovered the Zen of roller coaster riding. After all that terror, I felt safe in the fall.

My dad and I traveled to Kings Island together just once more, when I was 19 or 20. We rode The Beast again, as well as the original Bat. Vincent Price voiced the commercials for this new ride, so of course I had to ride it. On our first ride, my dad said that The Bat didn't feel right. I rode it several more times, alone. I've never experienced anything else quite like The Bat, and I'm sorry it's gone. Soaring through the trees in hanging gondolas felt like sitting in a front porch swing that had just taken to the skies at high speed. Oddly, it didn't scare me. Anyway, my dad and I agreed that The Beast was still the best ride, and that it was in the best park. My dad and I never returned to Kings Island together after that trip. Many of our best times together were spent there. We forgot our differences, relaxed, and had fun. If I had figured that out sooner, we might have gone back more.

Sheer Drop

During my 20s, 30s, and early 40s, my relation-ship with my dad grew more distant. He insisted that his retirement was "Heaven on earth." Yet he seemed more isolated and frustrated. He struggled to write and com-plained about interruptions. Eventually, though, he won some attention for his writing. He received a short story prize which included publication of one of his stories, and a state-of-the-art electric typewriter as well. In addition to stories and poems, he wrote long letters to me, expressing his mystical and philosophical views and offering a lot of confusing advice.

He felt proud that I had earned degrees in both Counseling and English Literature and eventually became a professor. He loved to brag about me to others, but when we were together, we had trouble talking. I was into English Literature and self-help books. He would lecture me about how I should read Bhagwan Shree Rajneesh or Carlos Castaneda. I didn't care for their particular brands of wisdom.

We could still have good discussions, but sometimes he would criticize, demean, or say mean things about our relatives, my friends, my mom, or me. When this happened, his bad language and ugly name calling upset and scared me. He would apologize later, in a letter or over the phone. I never understood what triggered these in-person outbursts, and eventually I chose not to stay with him at his home. Over time, my Aunt Jo and my mom shared with me that he had occasionally behaved in a similarly hostile way with them. My mom explained that this side of my dad, which many people never saw, was a factor in her decision to divorce him.

My dad's advice on relationships was particularly perplexing. Throughout my teens and twenties, he repeatedly told me never to get married. When I turned thirty, he asked me why my relationships with men never worked out, demanding to know what I was doing wrong. At the end of this conversation, he tried to soften his tone by conceding "Oh well, you've got ten good years left." Just a few months later, he drove from West Virginia to Illinois to visit me after I'd been through a difficult romantic breakup. He offered support and encouragement, taking me out to eat and to a movie, The Lion King. We had no ugly scenes. That visit meant a great deal to me. A few years later, another boyfriend moved with me to West Texas, where I had gotten a wonderful job on the faculty of an English Department. Later on, when this boyfriend moved out, my dad and Aunt Jo visited me in Texas to see how I was doing. We had a terrific time.

During the 1980's and 1990's my step-father and my mom moved around a lot because of Al's work, living in Chicago and Atlanta. In 1999, they moved back to Parkersburg, WV to retire. My mom and Al still bickered constantly and frequently had big arguments, but they were clearly still in love. I could once again visit all three of my parents in the same town! My entire family spent several remarkable Christmases together at my aunt Jo's wonderful little house, with my mom, Al, my dad, and cousins and their families, several large dogs, and a bird. Everyone got along beautifully for a few hours.

My dad and I never regained the closeness we had when I was young, but even when we were at odds, we said "I love you" at the end of each letter, phone call, or visit, and we meant it.

The final year of my dad's life, 2004, like our first trips to Kings Island, was filled with mix-ups and little miracles. In February, he underwent heart surgery that was supposed to be routine, but the procedure went poorly and ended in serious complications. I traveled to West Virginia for several days to visit him in ICU. Eventually, my dad was discharged to a nursing home for convalescence, but he declined steadily.

Just before Fathers Day, I found a website where I "purchased" a star to be named in his honor. A certificate and star chart showing his star's location would be mailed to him. This would make the perfect Father's Day present. The staff of the nursing home even told me that they would take him outside in his wheelchair and try to show him the star. But a few days before Father's Day, I received a call from the nursing home telling me about his death. My dad passed away and didn't ever see his star.

The next day, I received another call. "We have a problem." Surprised that there would be a new problem at this point, I listened as a nursing home staff member explained. My dad had chosen to leave his body to science, specifically, the West Virginia University cadaver lab. He did not want a gravestone or a funeral. He wanted to keep everything cheap and simple. "No funeral, no headstone, only a leaf has fallen," he wrote. This didn't surprise me, as I had heard him mention this plan. But his choice turned out to be more complicated than he expected.

The nursing home where he had passed was in Ohio, so his body was now in an Ohio morgue awaiting transport. However, the transporting of bodies across the state line was prohibited by law, so he couldn't be delivered to the lab in Morgantown, WV. So, one last time, with the help of the nursing home, I navigated. We made calls and filled out forms. Finally, his body arrived at its destination.

The next day, I went home to arrange a memorial service for him which took place on Father's Day, 2004. I decided to do this despite his wishes, for myself and for other people who wanted to say goodbye. My mom and stepfather helped me out through everything I needed to do. Going through his writing, I found a poem he wrote from the point of view of the painter Vincent Van Gogh to his brother, Theo.

Vincent

I painted myself to death.
Woke up in the east of Arles.
I know it was me. One ear gone.
One ear gone to the north,
And bark and twigs to the south.
West, a robin. Branches, clouds,
And endless, endless skies.
Tonight, I know, I will be stars!

And tomorrow, sunrise.
Theo, to see me now,
You'd not regret
The cost of paints and canvas.

Paul Harbin

"Vincent" poem by Paul Harbin. Calligraphy by Joan Harbin Rake.

I wonder if perhaps he knew about his star, after all. I put this poem on display for guests to view at his memorial. Polly, with whom I had lost touch, showed up at my mom and Al's house with a big pot of jambalaya and

49

a wonderful basket including some very welcome soothing bath products and a bottle of wine. Polly and I have stayed in touch ever since.

She and other dear friends helped me with his memorial service. Many people attended, including my mom, my step-father, and his ex-wife, as well as my second grade teacher, whom I had once hoped my dad would marry. Like those congenial Christmas gatherings, everyone came and everyone got along. People I'd never met told me how much Bud had meant to them. I planned to play several of his favorite songs, but the sound system I rented didn't work. So instead, we all sang "Raindrops Keep Falling on My Head." He would have liked that.

Twists and Turns

During the days in which I learned of my dad's death and held his memorial, I had a secret. Just a week before my dad's death in 2004, I was visiting my good friend Bob. We had an unexpected conversation.

Bob Hartlaub and I met thirteen years earlier, in the summer of 1991, at the Unitarian Universalist Congregation of Atlanta. I was 29 and he was 27. I was visiting Mom and Al, who lived in Atlanta at that time, before beginning my graduate studies.

Bob decided to visit the UU Church soon after moving to Atlanta, hoping to meet new friends. I decided to visit the same church, for the same reason, on the same beautiful summer morning. At the coffee hour, I was browsing some pamphlets. Crouching down to look at a pamphlet on the bottom shelf, I stepped back without looking behind me. Hearing a loud "Ouch!", I turned around to find a cute, sandy-haired guy with remarkable blue-green eyes whose hand was now under my foot and whose coffee was now on the floor. Mortified, I apologized. After we established that none of his fingers were broken, we mopped up the coffee and introduced ourselves. All this had attracted the attention of the leader of the Young Adults Group, who invited us to join their meeting. We did, then went out for lunch with them. We became friends that day and met for dinner several times that summer.

From the first, I knew Bob was special. After all, few people would have been so friendly to someone who had just stepped on their hand. I soon learned that he worked in IT for a large computer consulting company. He had lived in Wisconsin, Texas, California, and Ohio before Atlanta. A hard worker, he also knew how to relax, have fun, and enjoy life. He loved nature, travel, science fiction, movies, theater, and his extremely mellow cats, who would come running when he started his dust buster, allowing him to gently vacuum them. They would even roll over and let him vacuum their tummies! What kind of a man could inspire that much trust in a cat?

Bob grew up in a large Roman Catholic dairy farming family, later becoming a Deist. At the age of nine, Bob lost his father in a car accident. His mother remarried a few years later, so Bob gained a stepfather and step-siblings as a teen, just as I had. He joined Junior Achievement and, at 17, entered a competition in which members who sold 1,250 raffle tickets would win a trip to Hawaii. He quickly realized that some of his fellow members were enlisting the help of their parents to sell the tickets to their coworkers, giving them an edge that he considered unfair. He didn't have the same option, but by pounding the pavement every free minute house by house and also selling tickets to local businesses, he won that trip to Hawaii.

In college, he studied computer science and business, and after getting his degree he took a summer off to backpack around Europe alone, on a shoestring budget.

Like my stepfather, Bob has a great sense of direction. Like my dad, Bob is playful, fun-loving, and warm. They share a love of spontaneity and a tendency to lose track of time. Like both my stepfather and my dad, when Bob speaks, he often uses the wrong word or puts words in the wrong order, not realizing he has done so. This happens more if he's stressed or tired. I'd had plenty of practice with my dad and Al, so I usually understand him.

Bob and I enjoyed each other's company and became good friends. The Unitarian crowd kept us busy with movies, discussion groups, concerts, mini-golf, and other fun events. Many people in the group thought we were a couple, but we never dated. The summer of 1991 sped by. In August, I said my fond farewells to my new Atlanta friends, preparing to begin my busy new life as a graduate student in English.

Bob and I stayed in touch, seeing each other when I visited Atlanta and sending each other cards and notes. In 1993, Bob relocated from Atlanta to New York City. In 1999, I began teaching at a college in West Texas. During these years Bob began building his own IT consulting business and I was very busy teaching and writing. I dated, in hopes of finding a husband, but nothing ever worked out.

When my dating relationships broke up, I sometimes visited Bob in New York. We enjoyed Broadway shows, museums, restaurants, walks, and lengthy conversation. He had friends who worked in Broadway box offices and we were able to get some great seats. Until then I had only seen Broadway from the discount seats. What a thrill to really see the performers' faces! We once saw four shows in three days, packing in as many other attractions as possible in between.

When we crossed the busy Manhattan streets, Bob would grab my hand yelling, "We can make it!" We'd sprint into the traffic amid a cacophony of horns. I was alarmed, but I could run almost as fast as he could. I just figured every second mattered when you were trying to see a major museum exhibit between the two o'clock matinee and the eight o'clock curtain. This must be how people behaved in New York. We always had a great time together. I'd come home from these visits exhausted but happy. Bob said that I was one of the few people he knew who could keep up with him.

In August of 2001, on one of my visits, we took a harbor cruise, dancing and enjoying the Manhattan skyline. I photographed the World Trade Center, not knowing it would be for the last time. That September, Bob stood on Sixth Avenue watching the second tower fall. Over the next couple of years, he lost two close friends and his stepfather. After that, we talked more often and became closer.

On a visit in the spring of 2004, Bob stunned me. We'd returned to his apartment after show and were enjoying a nice glass of wine when he told me he had strong feelings for me that he'd been aware of for some time.

Over the years, we had talked a lot about our respective dating experiences and romantic relationships. Based on these conversations, I had concluded that I was definitely not his type. Now, as he told me that he had been waiting to catch me between boyfriends to tell me about his interest, I was more than delighted. I was also scared. Bob and I had been such good friends for thirteen years. What would this change mean?

The following week, my dad died. Over the next few days and weeks Bob and I agreed to keep our prospective romance a secret for a while, until we figured it out for ourselves.

I wanted a relationship with Bob, but this felt too good to be true. I was 42 and I was only interested in serious relationships. I needed to be sure he felt the same. We took our time. Over the next few months, we visited more. Eventually, we agreed that we both wanted a committed, long-term relationship. With each other!

For the next few years, our long-distance relationship went from being too good to be true to being truly hard work. Not surprisingly, we encountered plenty of challenges shifting from our years-long friendship to serious dating and eventual marriage. We became engaged in 2005 and married in 2006. I was 44 and Bob was 42. Our transition from friendship to marriage was the ride of my life, as full of exhilaration and fear as any roller coaster.

When he took me to Wisconsin to meet his huge family for the first time, we visited with a house full of relatives all afternoon. Tired from

Bob and Leigh about 2008

the flight and the hours of socializing, I was hoping for a quiet dinner with Bob and his mother, LaVerne. However, Bob explained that an evening out, with what he told me was "just a small group", had been arranged. Soon, a bus pulled up outside the house with Bob's four siblings, his four step-siblings, and their respective spouses all on board drinking champagne. Bob, LaVerne and I joined them. The bus took us to two bars, where the family knew everyone, then to a restaurant for dinner.

I tried to get into the party spirit, but I felt out of place. I had expected to get to know a lot of people, but they seemed more interested in talking to Bob and to each other. At dinner everyone decided it would be fun to throw ice cubes across the table, at each other and at me. We got to bed late and woke up early the next morning. I learned that Bob's family enjoys drinking more than I do and that they do not need sleep or meals on any predictable schedule. This only child was definitely overwhelmed and exhausted. Bob was disappointed.

We had a lot to figure out. Eating. Sleeping. Where to live? How to cross streets together? Bob preferred what I call the Evel Knievel approach: charging into oncoming traffic. This had been exciting on our brief visits, but it didn't work as regular practice for a nearsighted woman in her forties who still wore heels occasionally. I was afraid for my safety and raised my concerns at every corner. Literally. When you're walking in Manhattan, that means a lot of conversations.

Where would a woman struggling with her Christian faith and a Deist guy who mistrusted organized religion actually go to get married? How would the Atheists, Agnostics, Jews, Fundamentalist Christians, Catholics, Episcopalians, Unitarians, and Pagans, not to mention the Conservatives, Liberals, Farmers, Teachers, Computer Programmers, Classical Musicians, and Drag Queens that would make up the guest list at this wedding get along?

I wanted to bring all these people together and stage a big production. We wanted our friends and remaining parents to see us marry, so they'd believe it. Our mothers weren't getting any younger, so we knew we needed to get it done. My matron of honor admitted to me that she and her husband thought our wedding would never happen, but miraculously, it did. On July 1, 2006, Bob and I married in the Unitarian Universalist Church in Marietta, Ohio. It was smaller than the UU church in Atlanta where we met, but just as welcoming. We hosted a reception on a sternwheeler on the Ohio River, trapping everyone together for several hours.

An abundant buffet and an open bar soothed family and friends. Nobody fell, jumped, nor was thrown, overboard. We

Leigh Harbin and Bob Hartlaub
Wedding Picture 2006

were surprised by the arrival of a swarm of mayflies near the end of the evening—these winged insects descended in a cloud. Everyone dancing on deck began to slap at them, creating a new step for the occasion. Nevertheless, I think most everyone had fun that night, except for Bob and me. We were far too nervous. But we'd done it. We were married.

We spent our honeymoon at an historic resort hotel. A poor choice, as it turned out. We thought it would be relaxing, but we were bored: the place was lovely, but offered little to do except golf, which neither of us enjoyed. We should have gone to an amusement park, but it would take us a while longer to figure that out.

Returning to the city for the remainder of the summer, we felt crowded in Bob's one bedroom apartment, even if it was large by Manhattan standards. Professorships in English are scarce, and I was reluctant to leave my wonderful job and my three-bedroom house in Texas. Bob and his business partners were working hard building up their small IT company in New York, and it wasn't a good time for him to relocate. Besides, he had little desire to return to a smaller city after living in New York. We maintained a long-distance marriage for another two years, but I wanted to be with Bob. It didn't hurt that I had always loved New York, either. In 2008, I made the decision to leave my job and finally move in with my husband of two years. I knew I had a lot to learn, but I had no idea just how much

How Roller Coasters Saved My Marriage

I learned that being married is more work than being friends and that living in New York City is more work than visiting. Navigating the city, daily and on my own, excited me. It also scared me, although I was embarrassed to admit it. I applied for many jobs. I got a lot of interviews, but no full-time offers, so I became an adjunct instructor at several colleges. The challenge of understanding the differing needs of my students excited me, but I missed the sense of belonging at one institution and the progressing career that I'd enjoyed in Texas. As a tenured professor, I had felt like a big frog in a little pond. In NYC, I had become a tadpole in the ocean. Eventually, I mastered the subway and felt safer, but Bob often felt overly controlled by my limits.

I learned that like my dad and my mom and my stepfather, Bob and I were stubborn. Our comfort zones didn't always intersect. We could go from happy to furious in about two seconds. This scared me a lot more than getting lost in the city. I was afraid that we would end up fighting all the time, just as I had watched my mom fight through two marriages without ever figuring out how to stop. I had no model for how to be married without arguing.

Over time, Bob and I acquired two precious cats. I worried about our cats escaping from the apartment or falling out the window. We reorganized and redecorated our apartment. Eventually we acquired another apartment in our building, which became our home offices. This helped. Yet, we kept right on triggering each other. We were both just too stubborn to give up.

Over the next few years, I lost more people I loved. My wonderful Aunt Jo became ill with cancer, then passed away. My beautiful, intelligent, caring mom, who had also been my best friend, was diagnosed with Alzheimer's Disease. Her mild cognitive impairment had been apparent for years, but she maintained a long plateau in which it was easy to believe it would not get worse. I'm grateful that I was able to take my mom on several trips in her last years, to do things she chose. We even went to Dollywood on one of them, at her suggestion. She didn't want to ride anything, but she enjoyed the shows.

As my mom's illness worsened, I made more frequent trips to Parkersburg. I went alone a few times, but most often Bob came with me and supported me. My mother had designated me as her medical power of attorney and Al as executor, and he and I often disagreed about her care. We argued a lot, turning our anger at what was happening to her against each other.

In the midst of this mess, I grew to appreciate Bob more. He offered constant support and practical help. Together, we encouraged Al to use in-home aides and keep my mom at home as long as possible. Eventually, though, she needed round-the-clock care and her transition into a nursing home was extremely difficult. I felt deeply sad, angry, and guilty. During this dreadful time, as we made frequent trips from New York to Parkersburg together, Bob and I learned something new: we enjoy road trips together.

We drove rented cars through snowstorms and through abundant shared sunshine. We swapped memories. I told Bob about my trips with my dad and he told me about his travels with friends and family as a kid, visiting national parks and amusement parks. Eventually, we made a little time to be more spontaneous together. We found restaurants we loved and others we swore never to enter a second time. We noticed many places we'd like to explore. We didn't always have time to stop when Pigeon World or a haunted corn maze appeared on our path, but we learned that we both wanted to visit many of these attractions along the way, whether they were historically significant or just plain quirky. We decided to build in a little time to do fun things together, to try to offset some of the sadness and stress.

At Bob's suggestion, we visited the Flight 93 Memorial in Shanksville, Pennsylvania, followed later the same day by the nearby Johnstown Flood National Memorial in Salt Fork. These destinations, both powerful and deeply moving, certainly put our own problems into perspective, but could not really be called fun. September 11 still felt almost recent to both of us. The exhibits and film at Johnstown included plenty of gruesome detail. Furthermore, we just happened to arrive there on the anniversary of the flood, so the day ended with a display of glowing candles, one for each person who had died. While I appreciated the opportunity to learn so much about two of our nation's greatest tragedies in the same day, I told Bob that the next time he wanted to cheer me up, we should try something a bit more lighthearted. As a result, we agreed to visit Hershey Park. It was, after all, also on our way. We'd never been to an amusement park together.

As we entered the park, I started dithering. I fretted over where to carry my phone and my wallet. I found few rides I felt comfortable riding. The enormous new steel coaster with seats that left most of my body out in the open air intimidated me. I didn't want to ride such a massive coaster, especially with nothing but a lap bar. I wished for a shoulder harness. I wouldn't ride anything with inversions. Tight spinning makes me queasy. I was not a lot of fun. Here I was in my early fifties, more like my timid adolescent self than my late teen/early twenties self, who could ride and enjoy almost anything. Maybe I am just too old, I speculated.

Bob, on the other hand, wanted to ride everything! I spent a lot of time waiting for him to emerge from the exits of various rides, just as I had waited for my dad forty years earlier. I thought about my previous visit to Hershey Park many years before, on the rainy day when I had ridden fearlessly but alone. The park seemed more densely packed than I remembered, tracks intertwining like a roller coaster spaghetti bowl. I enjoyed watching people, something my mom also loved to do. I noticed how little time the guests at Hershey Park, especially the kids, spent on their phones. They were too busy deciding what to do, running from one ride to the next. That made me happy and glad we had come.

Bob and I rode the wooden coasters together and loved them, though they weren't as much fun as The Racer or The Beast. I loved the character of the wooden coasters. I felt safe in spite of the bumps and jerks because the cars surrounded me, and because I had so many great memories of them. As the day went on, I felt better and stopped fretting. We enjoyed some shows and the animals at Zoo America. Bob's enthusiasm for all the rides helped me rekindle my own. We talked about them even if I chose not to ride. We were not bored. In fact, we were having more fun than usual.

Later that year, as my mom's dementia progressed, Al decided to move himself and my mom to a care facility in Denver, near his daughter and his grandchildren. There, he lived in an assisted living apartment and my mom in a memory care unit. My mom still hated it, but at least they were together. Bob and I now made our visits by plane, and I saw my mom less often.

In November of 2015, she passed away. I attended her funeral in Denver, but I also arranged a memorial for friends and family in West Virginia in the spring of 2016. I wanted to honor her memory and celebrate her life in the place she had considered home. Many friends and family shared their memories of her. At the end of the service, we all sang "Somewhere Over the Rainbow," a favorite of hers that we sang together often when I was little. Al's health declined, and he passed away a little over a year later.

This was such a sad time that Bob and I didn't do anything special for our tenth anniversary in 2016. In 2017, though, we decided to treat ourselves with another visit to Hershey Park, this time with a stay at the Hotel Hershey. We loved the pampering and the food at this unique hotel, but mostly we loved the access to the amusement park. The coasters were calling us back! We went to Hershey Park daily. We continued to talk about which rides we enjoyed, which ones we didn't, and why.

One evening Bob and I took a stroll around the beautifully landscaped grounds. I was missing my mom, sad that I had never brought her to stay at Hotel Hershey. Feeling helpless about the last years of her life, I happened to look up at the sky and saw a gorgeous rainbow. I remembered singing "Somewhere Over the Rainbow" and tried to focus on our closeness. I miss my mom every day and always will, but this moment seemed like a sign of forgiveness and permission to begin to heal.

Our stay at Hotel Hershey passed quickly and Bob and I had a great time. We noticed that we hadn't had any arguments. That was more than we could say about our honeymoon years before, or most of our other trips, for that matter. We had a good laugh when one of us remarked that we should have spent our honeymoon at Hotel Hershey, instead of at the other historic resort with the golf courses. It only took us eleven years of marriage to figure that out.

Later that summer, Bob's work required him to travel to Cleveland, Ohio. I flew out to meet him so we could spend a few days at Cedar Point in Sandusky. We stayed at The Breakers Hotel at this historic park on Lake

Erie, where we found more roller coasters than we had ever seen in one place. On the first day of our visit, we checked in and relaxed in the colorful room. When we decided it was time to go to the park, we couldn't find the paper receipt we needed to get our entry passes. We didn't have an electronic copy! Near panic, we searched the room until we found the receipt behind the night stand, where it had fallen as we were unpacking. Much relieved, we headed for the park. Crisis averted, we noticed. We had worked together to find what we needed, without wasting time being angry.

At Cedar Point, I again spent much of my time waiting for Bob to emerge from exits, but I also decided to push myself a bit. I rode The Iron Dragon, a suspended coaster, hoping it would be like the original Bat at Kings Island. The Iron Dragon moved faster than The Bat but somehow didn't produce the same unique sensation of free flight that I remembered, but I enjoyed zipping through the trees and over the water, nonetheless.

I rode Maverick, despite its inversions, because it had a shoulder harness. Whoa—what a ride! By no means tame, Maverick helped me remember that I could handle inversions, even if they were not my favorite experience. I loved the powerful take off and remarkable speed of this bucking bronco of a coaster. Maverick helped restore some of my former confidence. I was getting a bit braver.

I enjoyed all the wooden coasters, even the enormous Mean Streak. I thought I might like Gate Keeper, but its wide wings with rows of suspended riders looked so fragile that I couldn't bring myself to try it. I also wouldn't ride Millennium Force, although it looked amazing, because I still couldn't deal with a 300-foot drop without a shoulder harness.

Bob absolutely loved Millennium Force, but he never pushed me to ride it. It was up to me now. So, I waited for him and, again, watched people interacting. I saw, as I had seen at Hershey Park, that folks weren't constantly on their cell phones. And neither were we. By the end of our stay, I knew I wanted to ride both Millennium Force and Gate Keeper. Next time.

Moreover, in the back of my mind, I kept thinking that a visit to Kings Island would be even better. I don't know why it took me so long to figure this out. Back in 2009, Bob had taken me to Paris. Gazing up for the first time at that older, bigger Eiffel Tower looming above me, I remembered my first view of the Eiffel Tower at Kings Island. I just didn't feel the same love for this one, even if it was, technically, the real thing. That should have been my first clue, but it took me nine more years.

My old favorite park just didn't happen to be in a place we had some other pressing reason to be. But that didn't mean we couldn't decide to go out of our way a little. Clearly, we needed more amusement parks in our lives.

In May of 2018, Bob and I visited Kings Island together for the first time. Excited as we pulled into the parking lot late in the afternoon, we couldn't wait to go in, but the skies looked gray. I remembered to note our row number, sad that it no longer had a cartoon character name. It was named for a coaster called Banshee that I'd never seen. What an excellent name for a roller coaster! My dad would have loved it! Would I ride it? I didn't know!

I did know Bob wasn't going to balk at the admission price. As we were approaching the park, he had already bought the season pass using his iPhone. Wisely, he suspected we'd be back and the pass would pay for itself. We got out of the car and headed toward the gate, but the weather had other plans. We were about ten steps from the car when the heavens opened. Lightning flashed and torrents of water gushed over pavement that had been dry moments before. So, we fled back to the car.

After checking into our hotel, we were tired. But the storm had cleared, and we couldn't wait until the next day. That evening we returned to the park for Skyline Chili, Graeter's ice cream, and a walk to look around. In the sunshine and fresh air after the storm, I felt almost blissful, and stayed very quiet. Bob clearly was thinking, "Who are you and what have you done with Leigh?"

Many things had changed, but so many things were the same. The view of the Royal Fountain and the Eiffel Tower still wowed me. When I saw the statue of Don Quixote and Sancho Panza on International Street, I felt a connection with my dad. He loved that statue. I'd forgotten all about it, and it brought back a flood of memories. He had told me about these two classic characters' adventures tilting windmills. And the log flume ride was still there! It seemed to belong to Snoopy now, but sharing the ride through the treetops with Bob felt amazing.

During the next few days, Bob and I rode all the wooden coasters. We loved The Racer, although it was bumpier than I remembered. We rode Adventure Express and met its massive tikis. Mystic Timbers' airy speed and the surprise in the shed was so much fun we rode it twice. I loved that these rides, added during my long absence, had such imaginative elements.

Of course, the greatest thrill was riding The Beast with Bob. Exactly as I had done 39 years before, I closed my eyes as The Beast dove down the drop into the tunnel, then opened them to marvel at the length of the ride and the way it works with the wooded terrain. Immediately, I rode a second time and kept my eyes open, feeling my entire body relax into the experience. As we sped through the woods, over the smaller hills, and descended the magnificent helix, the familiar feeling came back. I was amazed by how happy and calm I felt. Bob agreed that this was an utterly unique coaster.

I was too timid to ride Firehawk or Diamondback or The Banshee on that visit. But I kept thinking about them. We returned to Kings Island in August that same summer. I took my first ride on Diamondback, finally pushing myself to ride an enormous steel coaster with only a lap bar to hold me in place. Like my first ride on The Beast many years before, climbing Diamondback's lift hill I thought I'd made a big mistake. The incline was steep. My lap bar didn't seem tight enough. I was going to fall out for sure. I closed my eyes. When I didn't fall, I realized what a great ride it was, and I had to ride it again. I kept my eyes open the second time and have done so ever since. Once again I felt ready for anything.

So, I rode Mystic Timbers twice and Diamondback twice, then felt my heart racing and my stomach growing nauseous. I had to sit in the nearby air-conditioned restaurant for a couple of hours. I learned that at 56, I had to pace myself, but I could still conquer fear and have fun. I tried Firehawk and loved flying through the trees lying face down, well secured. The dreaded inversions didn't turn out to be so bad. Firehawk became a new favorite, one I wish my dad could have ridden. I'm sure he would have said it was "out of this world!".

Bob and I returned to Kings Island again in 2019, on a longer trip that also included visits to Kennywood, Holiday World, Cedar Point, and Dorney Park. We realized we wanted to visit more of these older parks, especially to ride historic coasters. The massive wooden coaster Mean Streak had been transformed into Steel Vengeance. This sprawling ride now sped over a steel track. Bob and I both loved this incredibly smooth, thrilling ride. We also just wandered around Cedar Point and took our time, really getting to know the park. We played games with the inhabitants of Adventure Island. We took breaks in the heat of the day to enjoy a swim in Lake Erie. One day, we sat out a rainstorm playing checkers on the porch of a shop in Frontier Town, until we played to a draw.

The following week, at Kings Island, we arrived for early entry, enjoying the welcome provided by a long-time park employee who led everyone in cheering for our favorite rides. We paused for our National Anthem and then raced through the park with the crowd. We both ran all the way from the gate to Diamondback. Bob filmed me on his phone. I looked like an old lady auditioning to be an extra in *Chariots of Fire*. We got in the short line for the front car. I had conquered my fear, holding my arms up in the air and delighting in soaring with only a lap bar to hold me down.

On that visit we rode all our favorites multiple times, remembering to take breaks and stay hydrated, of course. Bob even asked the attendant to let us wait for a brand new, bright red antique car, and we drove it around the gorgeous track that had opened that summer. That special ride felt quite romantic!

When traveling, we learned to take our time. We take turns driving and help each other stay alert. We listen to music or podcasts. We still have conflicts, but know that when we work against each other, we will come to a stalemate every time. Instead, we try to listen better and to focus on working *with* each other. When we work together to solve a problem, we usually figure it out. If we don't, we put if off if we can and try again later. This big improvement happened as we relearned how to have fun together.

Unexpected Stop

2020 was going to be our year to work differently and travel more. I had learned to teach online and Bob hoped to cut back his work time a little. We were eager to visit Cedar Point and Kings Island in the summer, enjoy all our favorite rides and experience Kings Island's new coaster, Orion. Then, we planned to add a fall trip, visiting Halloween Haunts at Kennywood, Cedar Point, and Kings Island, making stops at every haunted corn maze along the way. Well, as it turned out, we worked remotely all right, but our travel plans were canceled due to the Covid 19 pandemic.

In 2020, I learned that trusting my faith, trusting Bob, and trusting myself can still just be really hard. Sadly, Bob lost his mother, who passed away at the age of 96 after having been healthy most of her long life. I got used to teaching online, but I badly missed being in a classroom with students. My anxiety got stronger, but so did I, and so did my marriage.

I sometimes feel like a panicky kid who needs to talk to her mom, but can't. Therapy and prayer and Lexapro have helped me understand a few things. My parents did the best they could in tough situations, and so did I. I'm no longer a kid who needs to be pulled out of the river by strangers. Even if I don't always feel like one, I'm an adult with regrets, achievements, goals, and limited time on this planet. My husband can make me happy and he often does, but he's not responsible for my choices or my happiness. That's my job.

As we dealt with the losses and conflicts among our friends and families caused by illness and by politics, Bob and I faced real fears together instead of facing roller coaster drops and Halloween monsters. Thoughts of enjoying amusement parks in the future helped us cheer and encourage each other.

As I read these recollections, I'm surprised by how much they're about my fear, but I'm glad they're also about knowing that sometimes you can feel safe in the fall.

Getting Back in Line

In the summer of 2021, Bob and I returned to Cedar Point and Kings Island. I finally rode Millennium Force. I'm sorry I waited for so long to do so, and I'm very glad I got the chance. I'll be riding it again, I hope, even if I did feel light headed on the first drop. Oddly, even if I'm having an anxious day, my anxiety usually dissolves when I'm on a roller coaster. In our late fifties, Bob and I experience parks more as my dad would have in his fifties. We love to ride, walk, splash, and occasionally run, but we also love to relax.

In August 2021, we met and talked with many wonderful people. We visited with musicians after shows and with our fellow riders. Talking to people while waiting in line has become part of the fun. Sharing memories of our favorite parks and comparing our responses to new attractions brought us together with these folks. None of the problems in the world went away, but whether or not we saw eye to eye on every controversial issue didn't seem to matter nearly as much as how we were going to wait out the long line, whether the ride would stay open, whether everyone would get up the nerve to board, and where to go next. I still haven't ridden The Banshee because it closed down while we were in line. At least I got close. Maybe next time. I did ride Orion, twice. I wait for Bob while he rides Top Thrill Dragster at Cedar Point and Invertigo at Kings Island and that's just fine.

We're eager to visit more parks and experience more roller coasters, but The Beast remains my favorite. I feel connected to my dad when Bob and I stroll around Kings Island, especially when we look at Don Quixote and Sancho Panza on International Street. I'd like to think my dad is proud of me for riding new and bigger rides. I wish he could have met Bob and visited Kings Island with us, but I'm grateful for memories of my time there with him.

For me, Kings Island began as a magical oasis of fun and has grown into a healing, restorative place. Here, we can all enjoy putting down our phones and see each other while we scream our heads off. On our last visit, I saw a young man wearing a shirt that said "I stopped playing Minecraft to come here!" That says it all. So, Happy Birthday, Kings Island! Thank you for helping us have fun together. May you have a wonderful 50th, and many, many more!

ACKNOWLEDGMENTS

Many people helped to shape and improve this book. My conversations with them greatly increased my joy in writing it.

My colleague at the NYU School of Professional Studies, Bob Lamm, provided encouragement and practical advice. Bob's enthusiasm for personal writing gave me the push to finish the book. Elsa Peterson's thoughtful and thorough developmental edit improved the manuscript enormously. Dave Bass guided me through the experience of self-publishing with professionalism and humor. Without the three of you, this book likely would not exist. Many, many thanks.

So many wonderful conversations with employees and guests at Kings Island made me eager to tell this story. Alfred Freeman took time to talk with me at length about my idea of writing a personal Kings Island story, sharing his enthusiasm and knowledge of the park, as well as a wonderful video of vintage park footage. Evan Ponstingle autographed my copy of *Kings Island: A Ride Through Time* and offered further advice and encouragement. Thank you to everyone who has chatted with me about Kings Island.

Family and friends shared heartfelt responses and astute critiques. I am deeply grateful to Cassie Bosworth, Stuart Chen-Hayes, Dana Glossbrenner, Janie Harbin, Tina Hartlaub, Roger Jones, Saebra Pauley, Jeffrey Peterson, John Plausse, Janet Rogers, Robert Small, Polly Stephens, and John Watkins for reading drafts and providing invaluable feedback. Steven Morningstar read the manuscript and created the original cover art.

My brilliant husband, Bob Hartlaub, provided every possible kind of support: emotional, financial, technical, and editorial. He also did the laundry! His love, patience, and partnership enrich my life every day.

Our cat, Endora, waited, not so patiently, for me to finish writing and get back to petting her. She shows her interest in a book by nibbling off the top corner of its front cover. Dory, I hope you approve.

Finally, to anyone reading this story, thank you! I hope this book inspires you to relive your own Kings Island memories and to write about them.

Made in the USA
Middletown, DE
02 July 2022

68328137R00052